Workbook Publishing offers a range of evidence-based child and adolescent workbooks and treatment manuals.

MW01157128

To re-order this title, or to view our entire list of publications, visit our website www.workbookpublishing.com

Also available are:

- DVDs for training in the provision of the treatments,

- an interactive computer-assisted program (*Camp Cope-A-Lot*) using Cognitive-Behavioral Therapy to address anxiety in youth, and

- materials for youth with depression, anger management issues, and impulsivity.

THE COPING CAT WORKBOOK

Second edition

Philip C. Kendall, Ph.D., ABPP
&
Kristina A. Hedtke, M.A.

Temple University
Child and Adolescent Anxiety Disorders Clinic

The Coping Cat Workbook
Second Edition

ISBN-13: 978-1-888805-21-5
ISBN-10: 1-888805-21-8

Illustration and design by Robbi@robbibehr.com

This workbook benefited greatly from the input of numerous colleagues and clients. Special thanks to all trainees and professionals who have studied and worked within the Child and Adolescent Anxiety Disorders Clinic (CAADC). Also, the input of the many youth and their families who have participated in activities within CAADC is very much appreciated.

Printed in the United States of America

Workbook Publishing
P.O. Box 67
Ardmore, PA 19003-0067 USA
www.workbookpublishing.com

THiS BOOk BeIongs TO

_____

TABLE OF CONTENTS

TABLE OF CONTENTS

(continued)

APPENDICES:

SESSION 1: INTRODUCTION

Hi! My name is Coping Cat. Along with your therapist, we'll be working together for the next several weeks. Each time we meet, we'll be doing some tasks together. Now, this book may look like a lot to finish, but don't be alarmed. You won't be graded or tested on any of these tasks. Relax – we're going to try to have a good time while working together.

Before we get started, I want to introduce myself. I think it's easier to work with someone when you know a little about them. I'll start at the beginning. I was born on September 3, 1988. I have two sisters and three brothers. When I was only six weeks old, I was adopted by a nice family. Boy, was I scared when I first went to my new home! I even hid under the couch for awhile. It seemed like I was afraid of everything. I guess that's how I got the name Scaredy-Cat. I still get scared sometimes, but I've learned how to handle it.

Now you know a little about me. Let's find out about each other.

activities menu

★ Personal Facts Game

What is your therapist's first name?

_____

What is your therapist's middle name?

_____

When is his/her birthday?

_____

What is his/her favorite TV show?

_____

How many sisters or brothers does he/she have?

_____

Now make up three of your own questions and see if you can find out the answers.

1. _____
   _____

2. _____
   _____

3. _____
   _____

★ Games

Pick out a game or fun activity to play with your therapist.

introduction to feelings and thoughts

Throughout this workbook, we'll be talking about your feelings in different situations. Sometimes we'll talk about situations that you enjoy and at other times we'll talk about situations that make you feel nervous or scared.

Let's start off today with a situation that was fun. I want you to think of a time when you really enjoyed yourself. Take a minute to think. Got one? Great! Now that you've thought of the situation, I'd like you to describe it in the space below. Tell me what the situation was, how you felt and what you thought.

Feeling great!

Situation	Your Thoughts	Your Feelings
_____	_____	_____
_____	_____	_____
_____	_____	_____
_____	_____	_____
_____	_____	_____

Next describe a situation that happens on a typical day. Think of a time that was OK, not great but not bad either. Remember to say what the situation was and what you thought and how you felt.

normal Day

Situation	Your Thoughts	Your Feelings

Learning about S.T.i.C. tasks

We're going to end each session with an assignment we call a S.T.I.C. task. A S.T.I.C. task is something you can do to "Show That I Can (S.T.I.C.)." You will be learning lots of new things working with your therapist and doing this workbook. We want you to take what you learn with you and use those new skills in other situations. That's why we came up with the idea of S.T.I.C. tasks. They're your opportunity to practice what you've learned. Then at the beginning of each session, you can show your therapist what you have accomplished. It's your chance to boast!

Every time you do a S.T.I.C. task, you will receive 2 points or stickers that you can use to earn a reward. What kinds of rewards would you like to be able to earn? On page 73 you'll see a "Reward Menu." This is where you can list each reward and the number of points that it costs. After sessions 4, 8, 12, and 16, you can spend your points on some of the rewards you listed in the Reward Menu.

your S.T.i.C. Task for next Time...

1. Write an example of another time you felt really great--you weren't upset or worried. Remember to describe the situation you were in, what you were thinking, and how you were feeling.

Do this task on your own for next time. When you and your therapist discuss it next time you can earn 2 points, so be sure to remember!

3

S.T.i.C. Task · Session 1

Describe a time this week when you felt really great — when you weren't upset or worried. Remember to describe the situation you were in, what you were thinking, and what you were feeling.

_____

_____

_____

_____

_____

_____

_____

Do you remember what S.T.I.C. means?

S. _____

T. _____

i. _____

C. _____

SESSiON 2: recognizing feelings

How did you do on the S.T.I.C. task from last time we met?
(Discuss it, then record the points in the "bank" on page 72.)

activities menu

★ What Feelings do People Have?

This week we'll have some fun learning about the many different feelings that people can have and how to recognize these feelings in ourselves and others. Let's start by listing some different feelings you can think of on the lines below.

_____   _____

_____   _____

_____   _____

good job!

★ How do you know when...

someone's angry?

_____

someone's sad?

_____

someone's happy?

_____

someone's surprised?

_____

Now that you are thinking about feelings, think about this: Besides SAYING what they feel, how else do you know what someone is feeling?

Here's a question. How do you know when someone is angry? Can you think of two ways? Write your answer in the spaces below.

1. _____

   _____

2. _____

   _____

★ Match the Face with the Feeling

Many people show their feelings by the look on their faces. Others may show their feelings by what they do with their bodies. First, let's think about how people show their feelings in their faces. Let's try to figure out what feeling each of the following faces is showing and write the word for the feeling below the face.

★ Feelings Role Play: Can You Guess What I'm Feeling?

Try and show your feelings using only your face and body. No words! You can do it! See if your therapist can guess what you are feeling.

★ If I were in this situation I'd feel...

Read the following stories and write in a feeling that you might have.

Draw a face to show that feeling.

1. Your best friend comes running up to you on the playground. Your friend says, "Let's go play!"

   What feeling would you have?

   _____

   _____

Draw a face to show that feeling.

2. This week you and your class did a pretty good job on your assignments and were very well behaved and the teacher decided that you could all go on the school trip to the zoo. But on the day of the trip it is raining so the trip to the zoo is cancelled.

   What feeling would you have?

   _____

   _____

Draw a face to show that feeling.

3. You are at home and your parents are outside. You are the only one in the house — you hear a noise in the other room.

   What feeling would you have?

   _____

   _____

★ What are these people feeling?

Here are some drawings of different children and adults. Take a close look and think about how each person might be feeling. Write down one feeling for each person.

★ My therapist feels worried when...

Ask your therapist about a time he or she felt worried or scared. Find out how your therapist handled the situation.

★ Let's look at the situation cards or fear ladder.

On page 74-76, you'll find some "situation cards." They're labeled "easy," "medium," and "challenging." Whenever you think of a situation in which you feel only a little bit nervous or tense, write it in on one of the "easy" cards. If it would be really scary, write it in on one of the "challenging" cards. When you think of a situation in which you feel scared or worried, but it's not too easy or not too scary, write it on one of the "medium" cards.

If you want to, you can write the scary situations in the fear ladder on page 77 instead of using the situation cards. Your therapist can show you how.

recap ⋆

I'm sure you've got the idea now: you can tell a lot about feelings from expressions on people's faces and from other parts of their bodies. For example, you can sometimes show your feelings in the way you stand or sit, in where you put your hands, or how you hold your head.

your S.T.i.C. Task For next Time...

On the next page, write about 2 situations that happened to you. One situation should be a time when you felt really nervous, scared, or worried. The other situation should be a time when you felt relaxed. It's important to write about the situation as soon as you can, so you don't forget anything. Be sure to include details about what happened. Write down how you knew what you were feeling and the thoughts or feelings you had.

Write about two situations that happened to you this week. One situation should be a time when you felt really nervous, scared, or worried. The other situation should be a time when you felt relaxed. Remember to describe the situations, what you were thinking, and what you were feeling.

I was nervous, scared, or worried when _____

_____

_____

_____

I was relaxed when _____

_____

_____

_____

Watch someone else this week. It can be someone in your family, or a friend, or a TV character. How can you tell what this person is feeling if they don't tell you?

Name of other person: _____

Situation: _____

_____

_____

The other person's feeling: _____

_____

What did you see that was a clue to the other person's feelings?

_____

_____

_____

_____

SESSION 3: HOW DOES MY BODY REACT?

Today we're going to talk about the ways our bodies might react when we feel nervous. For example, as a cat, I show that I'm scared when my fur stands up. When I'm frightened, I feel like a Scaredy Cat.

Sometimes being afraid is ok – there are times when everyone is a little bit afraid. But, there are other times when we don't have to be afraid. When I keep my cool, I feel like I can cope with whatever comes my way. I'm a Coping Cat.

activities menu

★ How do my family members show that they're scared?

When people are scared, they can notice that their bodies give them clues or hints that they are scared. Think of a time when a family member or a friend of yours was scared. What ways could their bodies tell them that they were scared? Write them in the spaces below.

1. _____

_____

2. _____

_____

3. _____

_____

Draw a picture of a person who is feeling scared or worried.

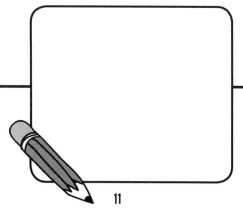

★ How do our bodies tell us we're anxious?

Look at the drawing of the human body below. Which part of your body gets a funny feeling when you feel nervous or worried? Draw a circle around it and describe how it feels.

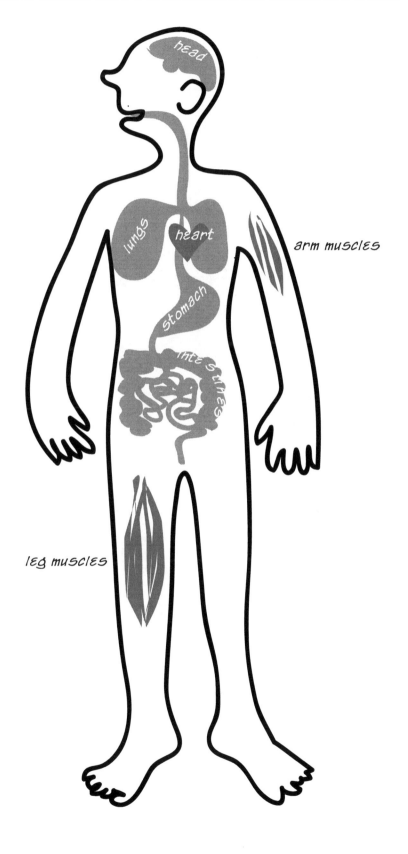

★ Let's answer some questions about how our body reacts

Sometimes there are several different reasons that could explain your feelings and how your body is reacting. Read the following situations and circle the number of the reason you think is the most likely why the person in the story feels the way he/she does.

Marina was very hungry, so she ate the tuna fish that had been in the fridge for several weeks. A few hours later her stomach feels upset.

Why do you think her stomach hurts?

1. The tuna fish was spoiled.
2. Somebody punched her.
3. She's worried about a test.

Terry is about to give a book report in front of his class. He notices that he feels sweaty.

Why might he feel that way?

1. He ran to school earlier that morning.
2. It's a hot day outside.
3. He's nervous about speaking in front of the class.

The last time Chris went to the dentist, he had to have a shot that hurt a little bit. Six months later he's in the dentist's waiting room again. When the dentist calls him to come and sit in the dentist's chair, Chris feels his heart beating really fast.

What could have caused his heart to beat so fast?

1. He swam in a race right before he went to the dentist.
2. He drank too much soda pop.
3. He was worried about what might happen with the dentist.

The answers to these three questions can help us to understand how our bodies give us clues. In Marina's situation, an upset stomach could result from any of the three reasons listed; but since we know that she ate very old tuna fish, we can be confident that the tuna fish upset her stomach. Keep in mind, though, that if her food was OK, a very important test could make her stomach upset.

Terry could be feeling sweaty because the air temperature is hot. However, if it is a cool day and if he hasn't been running within the last half hour, then his speaking in front of the class might be the cause of his sweating. Running, hot temperatures, and stressful circumstances all can make us sweat.

Chris felt nervous and he identified it when he noticed his heart pounding. He was worried about pain.

★ Let's learn the first step for coping with anxiety.

Recognizing that your body feels tense and that you're worried is the first step in learning how to cope with situations that make you anxious. To help myself remember this step, I call it

Feeling frightened?

Let's imagine that you're nervous. What's the first clue that you have that you're feeling anxious?

_____

_____

_____

Take a look back at all those feelings from session 2 (pages 5-9). People sure can feel a lot of different ways.

your *S.T.i.C.* Task for next time...

Draw your own rating scale to rate how your body feels in different situations.

During one day and evening, pay attention to how your body reacts when you feel different ways. See if you can tell how anxious you became by how strong the feelings inside your body were. Then use your rating scale to record how you felt about the situation.

Draw a rating scale to rate how your body feels in different situations.

my rating scale

Write down two times this week when you felt scared or worried, and give them a rating with your rating scale.

I was nervous, scared, or worried when _____

_____

_____

_____

RATING:

I was nervous, scared, or worried when _____

_____

_____

RATING:

SESSION 4: PARENT MEETING

activities menu

★ **Take the week off!**

You deserve it!!!

your *S.T.i.C.* task for next time...

Remember you're supposed to take the week off?
That means no S.T.I.C. task for this week!

SESSiON 5: LET'S ReLaX

Hi again! Today we're going to talk about how our bodies feel when they are relaxed and how they feel when they are tense.

activities menu

★ Robot/Ragdoll

Think of a time when you felt happy and relaxed. Imagine that you're in that situation. How does your body feel?

Now make a fist. Does it feel different than how your body felt when you were relaxed?

When I get tense, my body feels stiff like I'm a robot. Try to be stiff, just like a robot. My favorite robot is C3PO from Star Wars. Think of your favorite robot. I'll bet that you can walk like a robot walks. Just tighten your muscles and give it a try.

Next, I'd like you to relax all your muscles. Try to be floppy, like a rag doll. Pretend you are Raggedy Ann or Raggedy Andy.

Describe how you felt different when you pretended to be a robot and when you pretended to be a ragdoll.

_____   _____

_____   _____

_____   _____

_____   _____

★ Tense or relaxed?

Sometimes we can also notice when other people feel tense by the way their bodies work. Look at these pictures below. Can you rate how relaxed the cat feels? Under each picture note how tense or relaxed the cat is: place a "1" if the cat is relaxed, or if the cat is tense, put a "4".

1 = relaxed	2	3	4 = TENSE!

RATING:

RATING:

RATING:

RATING:

★ The muscles of the body.

Look at the picture showing the muscles of the human body. There are many different muscles... and they have long names! Some people are aware of their muscles only after they've used them, like if you've been writing or drawing for a long time, and suddenly your hand hurts. The muscles in your hand are tired. Or maybe you know someone whose neck hurts after a long and busy day. Sometimes after I've been watching birds, my tail is sore from twitching. Take a look at the picture and name the muscles. Point to each muscle on your own body. As you do, tighten that muscle so you can see how it feels.

Back

Biceps

Calf

Chest

Face

Feet

Forearm

Hands

Thigh

Neck

Rear End

Shoulders

Stomach

Triceps

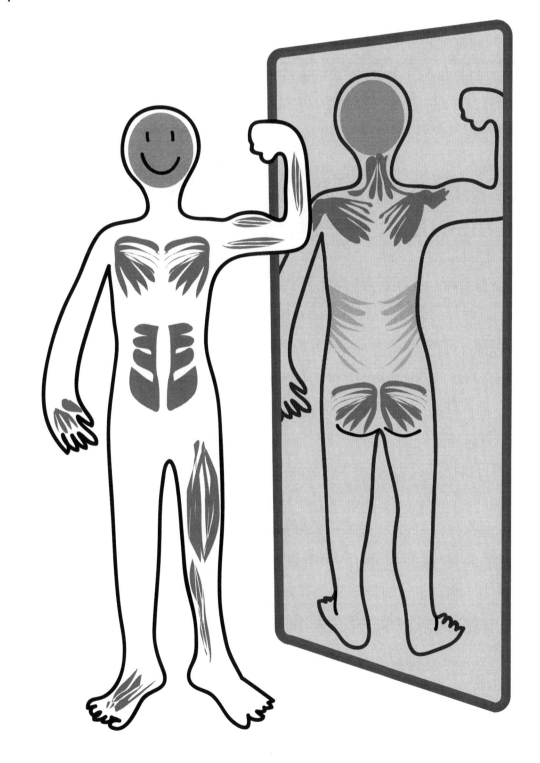

★ Learning to Relax.

Your therapist will teach you some relaxation exercises that can help you to feel relaxed at times when you are feeling worried, tense, or scared. You will get a tape that you can use to practice the relaxation at home.

your *S.T.i.C.* task for next time...

Try to relax at home. Then record your experiences with the relaxation in your notebook. This relaxation exercise will become easier the more you practice, so try to set aside some time every day. Write down the day and time then describe how you became relaxed. Also describe two experiences in which you felt nervous or scared. Record the thoughts you had and how your body felt.

S.T.i.C. task · session 5

Practice your relaxation every day at home. On two of the days, write down the day, the time, and how you became relaxed.

1. Day: _____   Time: _____

    I relaxed by _____

    _____

    _____

    _____

2. Day: _____   Time: _____

    I relaxed by _____

    _____

    _____

    _____

There's more on the next page! Keep going...!

Describe two times you were nervous or scared this week. Write down the situation and how your body felt, and then give the situation a rating using your rating scale.

Situation 1

I was nervous, scared, or worried when _____
_____
_____

Feeling frightened?

My body reacted by: _____
_____
_____

RATING:

Situation 2

I was nervous, scared, or worried when _____
_____
_____

Feeling frightened?

My body reacted by: _____
_____
_____

RATING:

SESSION 6: WHAT AM I THINKING?

In this session we're going to talk about the kinds of thoughts that people have in different situations. For example, if I won a catnip mouse at a raffle drawing, I would probably think "I'm so excited; I can't wait to play with it!" These thoughts are "talking to myself," so sometimes I call them self-talk.

activities menu

★ What's in the thought bubble?

This is a cartoon drawing of the Lincoln Memorial, a statue to memorialize one of the great Presidents of the United States. We call the balloon over his head a "thought bubble"—it's where the cartoon character's thoughts go. His thought bubble is empty. What might he be thinking? Take a minute to think, then turn the page for what he might be thinking.

I think Lincoln is stiff and cold from sitting on the hard seat!

He's thinking of a recliner. He wants to relax.

Now lets go on to some other situations. For each cartoon, take a look at the situation, then figure out what each person might be thinking. Fill in the thought bubbles. Go ahead!

Sometimes it's not that easy to tell what someone would have thought in a situation. In many situations, different people might have different thoughts. Let's consider the situation:

A teacher just announced that the class would be going to the roller rink. Let's meet two of the students in this class. Chris has taken roller blading lessons for a year and hopes someday to compete in contests. Terry went roller blading only once before, fell too many times to count, and went home with sore ankles. What do you think Chris and Terry would be thinking when they hear about the class trip? Do you think they would have similar thoughts or very different thoughts?

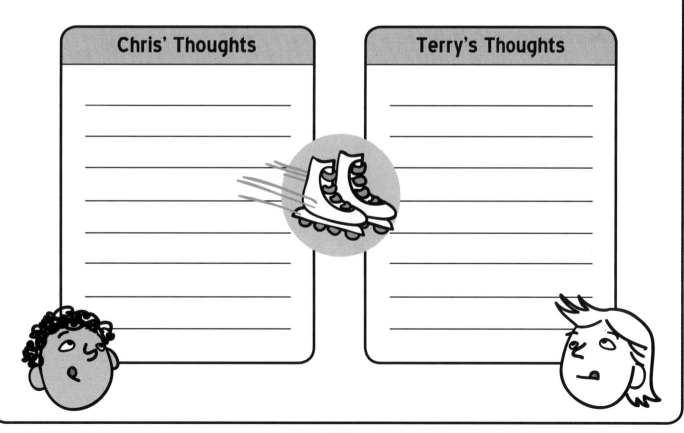

Chris' Thoughts

Terry's Thoughts

Now look at the cartoon below. This time the character has two thought bubbles. Try to think of two very different thoughts that the person might have. Write one in each bubble.

★ Different thoughts = different feelings and actions

How would the character in the cartoon above act and how would he feel if he had the thought in the first bubble? How would he act and feel if he had the second thought?

	Feeling	Action
Thought 1		

	Feeling	Action
Thought 2		

★ The second step.

Some types of thoughts can help people relax in the situation, while other thoughts might make people feel more nervous or scared. Take a look at this cartoon scene. Circle the cat that would be more frightened.

Why do you think that cat would feel more scared? _____

_____

_____

_____

Recognizing thoughts that might make you feel anxious or worried is the second step in our plan for coping with anxious feelings. I call this step

Feeling frightened?

Expecting bad things to happen?

★ Let's role play.

When I'm in a situation that makes me feel anxious, it helps me to notice what my thoughts are. For example, one day last spring as I was chasing a squirrel, I followed it up the tree in my backyard. I didn't catch the squirrel – I never do – but I was high up in the tree and suddenly felt really scared. I didn't think I would be able to climb down without falling. My thoughts were that I would be stuck in the tree forever. When I noticed what I was thinking I asked myself, "Is it likely that I won't be able to get down?" I remembered that I had climbed this tree several times before. Each time I had climbed the tree, I also had been able to climb down.

Think of a situation in which you felt a little nervous or scared. Imagine that you're in the situation and role play what happened.

your *S.T.i.C.* Task For next Time...

During the next week, write down two situations in which you felt scared or anxious. Pay special attention to the thoughts that you had and be sure to write them down also.

P.S. Don't forget to keep practicing your relaxation!

27

During this week, write down two times you felt scared or nervous.

Time 1

I was nervous, scared, or worried when _____

_____

_____

Feeling frightened?

My body reacted by _____

_____

_____

Expecting bad things to happen?

I was thinking _____

_____

Instead I thought _____

_____

Time 2

I was nervous, scared, or worried when _____

_____

_____

_____

There's more on the next page! Keep going...!

Time 2 · CONTINUED

Feeling frightened?

My body reacted by _____

_____

_____

Expecting bad things to happen?

I was thinking _____

_____

Instead I thought _____

_____

Practice your relaxation. Describe what happened. What was it like?

Day: _____   Time: _____

I relaxed by _____

_____

_____

_____

Hi again! Do you remember how we start each session? That's right, with a review of your S.T.I.C. task. Let's review what you wrote and give you the points you earned!

activities menu

★ Let's learn the third step.

What we've learned in the last session is how to recognize our self-talk. That is the second step in our plan for coping with anxiety. If you remember, we called this step "Expecting Bad Things to Happen?" The more you practice noticing your self-talk, the more you'll know what you're expecting. Today we will be learning a third step in the plan I use to help myself cope with worry. So far, you have learned how to recognize when you're feeling anxious and how to recognize your self talk. Now let's talk about what you can do when you feel scared or nervous. How can we use what we've learned so far to be less scared, more relaxed, and have a good time? I call this step

Feeling frightened?

Expecting bad things to happen?

Attitudes and actions that can help

If you look in the back on page 80 you'll see a page titled "Attitudes and Actions." Whenever you have an idea about an attitude or action that can help you cope, write it on that page. Then if you need some ideas, you can always look at this list. I think it's so helpful to write things down!

★ How do the steps help?

Here is a situation that we can use as an example:

There is a new kid in class that you would like to get to know, but you feel nervous about talking to him. He sits down next to you in the cafeteria. What do you do?

1. **F**eeling frightened?

Are you feeling nervous? How can you tell? _____

_____

_____

_____

_____

2. **E**xpecting bad things to happen?

Tune into your self-talk — what is it that is worrying you in the situation? Using the example, write down your ideas.

_____

_____

_____

_____

3. **A**ttitudes and actions

Now list some of the possible things you could do. Ask yourself "What can I do to make this situation less fearful?"

1. _____

_____

2. _____

_____

3. _____

_____

Next you need to choose the best ideas for you. Focus on each possibility. Ask yourself:

"What might happen if I chose the first idea?" _____

_____

_____

"How would I feel?" _____

_____

_____

_____

Now we'll go through the same process with your second and third possibilities. Ask yourself:

"What might happen if I chose the second idea?" _____

_____

_____

"How would I feel?" _____

_____

_____

_____

Ask yourself: "What might happen if I chose the third solution?" _____

_____

_____

"How would I feel?" _____

_____

_____

_____

Now you have thought about each possibility.
Which one do you think might be the best one for you?

_____

_____

good job!

32

Now think of a situation that would make you feel anxious or scared. Write it down in the space below. Then use the three steps to cope.

Situation: _____

_____

_____

Your Feelings	Your Thoughts	Your Actions
_____	_____	_____
_____	_____	_____
_____	_____	_____
_____	_____	_____
_____	_____	_____
_____	_____	_____
_____	_____	_____

recap ·

We've learned many new things during the time we've spent together. I think we should take a few minutes to review. So far, we have learned several ideas that can be helpful when we feel anxious. On the next page, write down two things that you've learned so far.

Two things I've learned so far:

1. _____
_____
_____
_____
_____
_____

2. _____
_____
_____
_____
_____

Let's Review!

your S.T.i.C. Task For Next Time...

Before our next meeting write down two situations in which you felt anxious, but then used the skills you've learned. Describe what happened in each situation and how you used the skills.

During this week, write down two times you felt scared or nervous.

Time 1

I was nervous, scared, or worried when _____

_____

_____

Feeling frightened?

My body reacted by _____

_____

_____

Expecting bad things to happen?

I was thinking _____

_____

_____

Instead I thought _____

_____

_____

Attitudes and actions that can help

What helped me was _____

_____

_____

There's more on the next page! Keep going...!

Time 2

I was nervous, scared, or worried when _____

_____

_____

Feeling frightened?

My body reacted by _____

_____

_____

Expecting bad things to happen?

I was thinking _____

_____

_____

Instead I thought _____

_____

_____

Attitudes and actions that can help

What helped me was _____

_____

_____

_____

_____

good job!!

36

SESSION 8: HOW AM I DOING?

Welcome back! Today we are going to learn the last step in our plan for coping with anxiety. We can call this step

Feeling frightened?

Expecting bad things to happen?

Attitudes and actions that can help

Results and rewards

activities menu

★ **What's a reward?**

I'll bet you can describe what reward means!

_____

_____

List some different types of rewards. Nothing too big or expensive. Small rewards can make us feel good too.

1. _____   4. _____

2. _____   5. _____

3. _____   6. _____

Good! Sometimes I get rewarded by other people, but I also rate myself and, when I'm happy with how I did, I'll reward myself. Often times I'll tell myself "Hey, I did a good job." Even when things don't turn out perfectly, I try to reward myself for what I did do well. For example, I might reward myself by spending some extra time grooming.

★ Let's practice using the results and rewards step.

Anika is playing for her school soccer team and scores a goal. What could Anika say to herself for a reward?

_____

_____

Jeff wrote an essay for a city contest and won 3rd prize. How should Jeff reward himself?

_____

_____

★ Rewards aren't just for perfect jobs.

Sometimes, even if I do a good job, things don't work out exactly the way I planned. Or sometimes I think I could have done a better job. In those cases, I still try to reward myself for what I did do well. After all, we can't be perfect!

Like when I made a cake for my friend, but forgot to take it out of the oven on time and it burned. I was still pleased with myself for thinking of my friend on his birthday, even though the cake wasn't perfect.

Think of an OK result, not perfect, but not terrible either. What might be in the thought bubble of a person in that situation?

_____

_____

_____

_____

_____

_____

★ Try the Feelings Barometer

Now why don't you practice rating yourself. Turn to page 78 and cut out the "Feelings Barometer."

1. Imagine yourself in this situation: You have been having some trouble understanding your math homework. You work hard and finally figure it out. Using the "Feelings Barometer," rate how you would feel.

2. Make up a situation of your own and write it down here.

_____

_____

_____

_____

Using the "Feelings Barometer" rate yourself again.

3. OK, let's try a tougher situation.

_____

_____

_____

_____

Using the "Feelings Barometer" rate yourself again.

We've learned a lot so far! We've learned a 4-step plan that can help us cope when we feel anxious. Sometimes, especially when I'm feeling nervous, I'll have trouble remembering a step. It's easier for me to remember things if I can think of a trick that will give me a clue. To help myself remember the 4-step plan, I think of the word FEAR. Each letter of the word stands for the first letter of the steps.

★ Make your own FEAR plan card.

Now that we have learned all four of the FEAR steps, turn to page 79. Cut out the card that you find on that page. On the card, write the four steps for coping with anxiety. Decorate the card any way you like. You can refer to this card whenever you feel anxious and need to remind yourself of the steps to use.

★ A coping character.

When I'm coping with a tough situation, it helps me to think of a storybook or cartoon character who would handle the situation well. I can think about how that person would cope and that gives me an idea of how I should try to cope. I'd like you to think of a character from a comic strip, book, or TV show that would help you to feel calm. If you can't think of anyone, make up a character. Describe your character on the lines below.

_____

_____

_____

_____

_____

_____

your S.T.i.C. task for next time...

1. Record two situations in which you felt anxious and you used the steps we've learned to help yourself cope with anxiety. Describe how you rated yourself on how well you've coped. Also describe how you rewarded yourself for coping with the situations. Be sure to reward yourself for partial success, not just for total success.

2. Show the card that you made to a parent and explain the steps to them.

During this week, write down two times you felt scared or nervous.

Time 1

I was nervous, scared, or worried when _____
_____
_____

Feeling frightened?

My body reacted by _____
_____
_____

Expecting bad things to happen?

I was thinking _____
_____
_____

Instead I thought _____
_____
_____

Attitudes and actions that can help

What helped me was _____
_____
_____

Results and rewards

How did I do? _____

I rewarded myself by _____
_____

There's more on the next page! Keep going...!

Time 2

I was nervous, scared, or worried when _____
_____
_____

Feeling frightened?

My body reacted by _____
_____
_____

Expecting bad things to happen?

I was thinking _____
_____
_____

Instead I thought _____
_____
_____

Attitudes and actions that can help

What helped me was _____
_____
_____

Results and rewards

How did I do? _____
I rewarded myself by _____
_____

Don't forget to teach a parent the FEAR steps. You can use your FEAR card to help!

SESSION 9: PARENT MEETING

activities menu

★ **Take the week off!**

You deserve it!!!

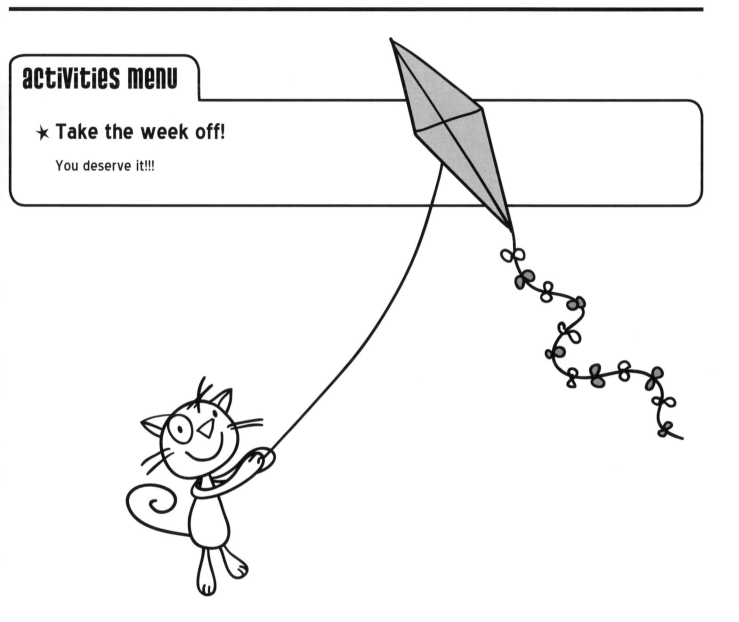

your S.T.i.C. task for next time...

Remember you're supposed to take the week off?
That means no S.T.I.C. task for this week!

SESSION 10:START PRACTICING!

activities menu

★ Remember the FEAR plan?

First, a quick review. Write down the FEAR plan below. If you can, write it down without looking at your clue card.

F _____

E _____

A _____

R _____

★ It's time to start practicing.

Turn to the situation cards on page 74 or the fear ladder on page 77. Pick one of the easy situations. Write down a plan for coping with this situation using the FEAR plan.

F _____
_____

E _____
_____

A _____
_____

R _____
_____

★ Let's role play

Using the plan you've developed, role play this situation with your therapist.

★ Rate your level of anxiety

Before each situation that you try out, I'd like you to rate how nervous or relaxed you'll be. Let's come up with a scale for you to use. For example, "0" could be very relaxed, and "8" could be extremely nervous or scared. These are already written in. Now you can add a description for "3" and "5" under the numbers.

very relaxed   very worried

_____   _____

_____   _____

_____   _____

good job!

your S.T.i.C. task for next time...

1. Practice using the FEAR plan in one easy situation that makes you feel a little anxious.

2. Draw or cut out a picture of your favorite cartoon character who can help you cope when you feel anxious. Bring the drawing or cut out to our next session.

Practice one time using "the _____ steps".

I practiced by _____

_____

_____

Feeling frightened?

My body reacted by _____

_____

_____

Expecting bad things to happen?

I was thinking _____

_____

_____

Instead I thought _____

_____

_____

Attitudes and actions that can help

What helped me was _____

_____

_____

Results and rewards

How did I do? _____

I rewarded myself by _____

_____

There's more on the next page! Keep going...!

Have some fun! Draw or cut out a cartoon character who you can think of when you want to cope with feeling anxious.

SESSION 11: MORE PRACTICE

activities menu

★ **Practice an easy situation**

Turn to page 74 (or page 77) and pick another easy situation. Using that situation, draw and write a cartoon strip that shows how your cartoon character would cope.

★ **Let's pretend we're actors**

Role play the situation you just drew. Imagine that you are really in the situation. This is your chance to be an actor!

★ **Another easy situation**

Again, turn to page 74 (or page 77) and pick another situation. Think of some reasons that someone might feel nervous in that situation. List two reasons:

1. _____
   _____

2. _____
   _____

Let's make a plan to cope with the situation you just picked.

F _____
_____

E _____
_____

A _____
_____

R _____
_____

★ Practice another situation

Rate how nervous you think you'll feel when you practice using the plan you just made to cope. Use the scale below.

0 **1** **2** **3** **4** **5** **6** **7** **8**

After you practice using your FEAR plan, record the thoughts and feelings you had during the situation.

_____

_____

_____

your S.T.i.C. task for next time...

Practice using the FEAR plan in two situations that make you feel a little anxious. Describe each step of the plan as you used it.

49

S.T.i.C. Task · Session 11

Practice two times using "the _____ steps".

I practiced by _____

_____

_____

Feeling frightened?

My body reacted by _____

_____

_____

Expecting bad things to happen?

I was thinking _____

_____

_____

_____

Instead I thought _____

_____

_____

Attitudes and actions that can help

What helped me was _____

_____

_____

Results and rewards

How did I do? _____

I rewarded myself by _____

_____

There's more on the next page! Keep going...!

I practiced by _____

_____

_____

Feeling frightened?

My body reacted by _____

_____

_____

Expecting bad things to happen?

I was thinking _____

_____

_____

Instead I thought _____

_____

_____

Attitudes and actions that can help

What helped me was _____

_____

_____

Results and rewards

How did I do? _____

I rewarded myself by _____

_____

Welcome back!

SESSION 12: MORE PRACTICE

★ **Medium situations: not easy, but not too challenging either!**

Turn to page 75 (or page 77) and pick one of the medium situations. In one of these situations I would probably look like this:

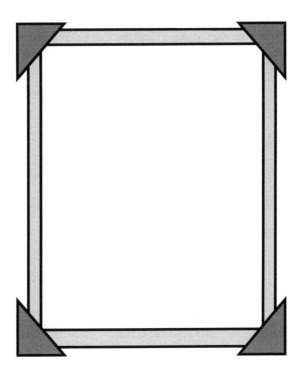

Describe how you might feel in this situation.

_____

_____

_____

_____

_____

Sometimes there might be several things that could cause you to worry in a situation. Think of all the things that might make you feel nervous in the situation you picked and how you would cope with each one.

_____

_____

_____

_____

_____

_____

_____

_____

_____

_____

Act out the situation.

★ Practice a real situation

Now let's really practice in the same situation. First, let's make a plan.

F _____

E _____

A _____

R _____

_____

Before we practice the situation, rate how nervous you think you'll be.

0 1 2 3 4 5 6 7 8

After you practice using your coping plan, record the thoughts and feelings you had during the situation.

_____

_____

_____

_____

_____

_____

_____

_____

_____

your *S.T.i.C.* Task For next Time...

1. Practice using the FEAR plan in two situations that make you feel anxious. Describe each step of the plan as you used it.

2. Remember the cartoon character you drew for Session 10? Make up a story about how that character could help children cope in a situation like one that might make you feel anxious. Be prepared to tell your story next time we meet.

S.T.i.C. Task · Session 12

Practice two times using "the _____ steps".

I practiced by _____

_____

_____

Feeling frightened?

My body reacted by _____

_____

_____

Expecting bad things to happen?

I was thinking _____

_____

_____

Instead I thought _____

_____

_____

Attitudes and actions that can help

What helped me was _____

_____

_____

Results and rewards

How did I do? _____

I rewarded myself by _____

_____

There's more on the next page! Keep going...!

I practiced by _____

_____

_____

Feeling frightened?

My body reacted by _____

_____

_____

Expecting bad things to happen?

I was thinking _____

_____

_____

Instead I thought _____

_____

_____

Attitudes and actions that can help

What helped me was _____

_____

_____

Results and rewards

How did I do? _____

I rewarded myself by _____

_____

Don't forget to make up a story about how your cartoon character could help children cope in a situation that might make them anxious!

SESSION 13: IT'S GETTING TOUGHER

Today you'll get a chance to practice some more. You will try out a situation that will be moderately scary. It won't be real easy, but it won't be too hard either.

activities menu

★ A scary situation

First pick a situation from page 75 (or page 77). Think of the scale from 0 to 8. Using that scale, pick a situation that would be a 4.

Using the FEAR plan, describe how you would cope with the situation.

F _____

_____

E _____

_____

A _____

_____

R _____

_____

Role play the situation with your therapist, then describe how it went.

Thoughts	Feelings	Results
_____	_____	_____
_____	_____	_____
_____	_____	_____
_____	_____	_____

★ Practice a real situation

Select a situation with your therapist and then make a plan.

F _____

_____

E _____

_____

A _____

_____

R _____

_____

_____

Rate how nervous you think you'll be by circling the appropriate number below.

0 **1** **2** **3** **4** **5** **6** **7** **8**

Record the thoughts and feelings you had during the situation.

_____

_____

_____

_____

your S.T.i.C. Task for next time...

Practice using the FEAR plan in two situations that make you feel anxious.

Practice two times using "the _____ steps".

I practiced by _____

_____

_____

Feeling frightened?

My body reacted by _____

_____

_____

Expecting bad things to happen?

I was thinking _____

_____

_____

Instead I thought _____

_____

_____

Attitudes and actions that can help

What helped me was _____

_____

_____

Results and rewards

How did I do? _____

I rewarded myself by _____

_____

There's more on the next page! Keep going...!

I practiced by _____

_____

_____

Feeling frightened?

My body reacted by _____

_____

_____

Expecting bad things to happen?

I was thinking _____

_____

_____

Instead I thought _____

_____

_____

Attitudes and actions that can help

What helped me was _____

_____

_____

Results and rewards

How did I do? _____

I rewarded myself by _____

_____

SESSiON 14: LET'S PRACTiCE SOME MORE

★ A challenging situation

Turn to page 76 (or page 77) and pick a situation that could cause lots of anxiety. Describe how you could cope in this situation.

_____

_____

_____

_____

How well do you think your plan would work?

_____

_____

_____

Go ahead and try it out in a role play.

★ Let's practice

Select a situation with your therapist and then make a plan.

F _____

E _____

A _____

R _____

_____

Rate how nervous you think you'll be by circling the appropriate number below.

0   1   2   3   4   5   6   7   8

After you practice using your coping plan, record the thoughts and feelings you had during the situation.

_____

_____

_____

_____

_____

_____

_____

Your S.T.I.C. Task For Next Time...

1. Practice using the FEAR plan in two situations that make you feel anxious. Write down things that made you anxious and how you coped.

2. Start thinking about a commercial in which you can show other people how to cope with a scary situation. You could feature your cartoon character if you like. It could be a radio, TV, or newspaper commercial, or you could write song lyrics or a poem. Your choice.

Practice two times using "the _____ steps".

I practiced by _____

_____

_____

Feeling frightened?

My body reacted by _____

_____

_____

Expecting bad things to happen?

I was thinking _____

_____

_____

Instead I thought _____

_____

_____

Attitudes and actions that can help

What helped me was _____

_____

_____

Results and rewards

How did I do? _____

I rewarded myself by _____

_____

There's more on the next page! Keep going...!

I practiced by _____

_____

_____

Feeling frightened?

My body reacted by _____

_____

_____

Expecting bad things to happen?

I was thinking _____

_____

_____

Instead I thought _____

_____

_____

Attitudes and actions that can help

What helped me was _____

_____

_____

Results and rewards

How did I do? _____

I rewarded myself by _____

_____

Don't forget to be thinking about your commercial!

good job!

SESSION 15: ANOTHER CHANCE TO PRACTICE

Today we'll spend some time working on your ideas for your commercial!

activities menu

★ Commercial ideas

Remember we talked about your doing an ad or song or poem or whatever to teach others how to cope with anxiety. Use the space below to do some sketches or write down some ideas.

★ Time to practice

Let's practice another situation today that makes you feel very anxious. Write the situation down.

_____

_____

_____

_____

_____

_____

_____

Now imagine a character in that situation who would probably really mess up. What is the worst thing that could happen to the character? Describe what might happen below.

_____

_____

_____

_____

_____

_____

_____

What suggestions could you give that character that might help him in the situation?

_____

_____

_____

_____

_____

_____

_____

_____

Finally, describe how you would handle the situation using the coping skills outlined in the FEAR plan.

F _____

E _____
_____

A _____
_____

R _____
_____

Rate how fearful or worried you think you'll feel by circling the number below. Go ahead and try out the situation.

0 1 2 3 4 5 6 7 8

After you practice using your coping plan, record the thoughts and feelings you had during the situation.

_____
_____
_____
_____
_____

your S.T.i.C. Task for next Time...

1. Practice using the FEAR plan in two situations that make you feel anxious. Describe how you used the FEAR plan to cope with your anxiety.

2. Prepare any materials you will need to do your commercial in the next session.

Practice two times using "the _____ steps".

I practiced by _____

_____

_____

Feeling frightened?

My body reacted by _____

_____

_____

Expecting bad things to happen?

I was thinking _____

_____

_____

Instead I thought _____

_____

_____

Attitudes and actions that can help

What helped me was _____

_____

_____

Results and rewards

How did I do? _____

I rewarded myself by _____

_____

There's more on the next page! Keep going...!

I practiced by _____

_____

_____

Feeling frightened?

My body reacted by _____

_____

_____

Expecting bad things to happen?

I was thinking _____

_____

_____

Instead I thought _____

_____

_____

Attitudes and actions that can help

What helped me was _____

_____

_____

Results and rewards

How did I do? _____

I rewarded myself by _____

_____

Don't forget to bring in any props or materials you might need to make your commercial!

SESSiON 16: YOU DiD iT!!

Boy, we've learned a lot in the time we've worked together. You have a plan for coping with fearful or anxious experiences, and you've had lots of practice. How well have you done?

activities menu

★ Let's practice!

Let's practice one last time using the FEAR steps in a challenging situation. Turn to page 76 (or page 77) and pick a situation that could cause lots of anxiety. First make a plan and describe how you could cope in this situation.

F _____

_____

E _____

_____

A _____

_____

R _____

_____

How well do you think your plan would work?

_____

_____

_____

Remember to rate the amount of worry or fear you think you'll feel.

0 **1** **2** **3** **4** **5** **6** **7** **8**

After you practice using your coping plan, record the thoughts and feelings you had during the situation.

_____

_____

_____

_____

_____

★ Now let's have fun!

You get to do or show your therapist your commercial.

Cash in any points you have left and enjoy the rewards. You earned them!

Receive your certificate of achievement (page 81) and be proud.

recap ⋆

Remember, you can use the FEAR plan we've practiced to cope with anxious situations that come up in the future. Good luck!

Congratulations! You completed all of the S.T.I.C. Tasks. You did it! You can use the rest of this book to keep practicing the FEAR steps at home.

THE BANK

SESSION 1	SESSION 2	SESSION 3	SESSION 4
			FreeBie!!

SESSION 5	SESSION 6	SESSION 7	SESSION 8

SESSION 9	SESSION 10	SESSION 11	SESSION 12
FreeBie!!			

SESSION 13	SESSION 14	SESSION 15	SESSION 16

reward menu

reward	Number of points or stickers

73

SITUATION CARDS ★ EASY

easy	easy
easy	easy
easy	easy
easy	easy
easy	easy

SITUATION CARDS ★ MEDIUM

medium	medium
medium	medium
medium	medium
medium	medium
medium	medium

SITUATION CARDS ★ CHALLENGING

challenging	challenging
challenging	challenging
challenging	challenging
challenging	challenging
challenging	challenging

Fear Ladder

You're up there...!

Getting higher...

too high...

aTTiTuDes	aCTioNs